MEL BAY PRESENTS

WARM-UPS FOR THE VIOLINIST

BY CAROL ANN WHEELER

QWIKGUIDE®

1 2 3 4 5 6 7 8 9 0

Visit us on the Web at www.melbay.com – E-mail us at email@melbay.com

About the Author

Carol Ann Wheeler has an extensive background of over 20 years as a violinist, orchestral member, and string teacher for public and private schools. She has always been fascinated by the sound of the fiddle. In 1974 she began to study and learn how to play old–time fiddle. Intrigued by different styles of fiddling she became a collector and performer of several: old–time, Texas, trick and show fiddling, cross tunes, Canadian, Scottish, and Irish to list some of the styles she enjoys. Since 1974 she has produced five fiddle albums and has been a contest fiddler, performer, judge, and fiddle workshop teacher. She performed for ten years through Young Audiences of Oregon and Washington, and has traveled and performed in Japan, Canada, and Scotland, as well as the U.S.

Mrs. Wheeler taught her own two children (who both became champion fiddlers) how to play fiddle, starting them at very young ages. Her home contains over 200 fiddle–contest trophies, plaques, etc. Through her books, fiddle workshops, albums, and performances, she has taught and perpetuated fiddle music to thousands. She and her students have won numerous times on the state, regional, and national levels. As announcer Harry Reeves said at the National Fiddle Contest in Weiser, Idaho, "You name it, she's won it!"

Mrs. Wheeler is known for being an energetic and enthusiastic performer and for teaching not just notes, but technique and style as well. She is thrilled to be able to reach and perpetuate the art of old–time fiddling to an even larger scope of people through Mel Bay Publications.

Credits

Many thanks to:

Steve Lawrence, of **Steve Lawrence Phone Co.**, as recording engineer and production assistant.

Linda Danielson, my twin–fiddle partner, for proofreading the text, and for help and encouragement through the years.

And very special thanks to my wonderful parents for all the help, patience, and support in putting up with my "fiddle madness" for the past several years.

Foreword

Over the years of listening to Carol Ann Wheeler, occasionally team–teaching workshops or sharing the stage with her, and recording *The Joy of Twin Fiddling* together, I've had plenty of opportunity to marvel at her consistently beautiful tone and dextrous fingers. I couldn't even tell you how many times I've heard aspiring fiddlers say to Carol Ann, "How do you get such clarity?" Or "What's the secret of your great tone?" Or "I want to sound just like you."

Actually, no one will ever sound just like someone else, and that's one of the delights of fiddling. Moreover, no magic prescription or instant fix will produce dexterity or luscious tone. But a common–sense principle is at work here: If you want quality sound or great facility, find out what the good fiddlers do to achieve their goals, and try some of their methods. You have an opportunity to do this by using *Warm–Ups for the Violinist*.

Carol Ann is publishing *Warm–Ups* because the method works. Designed especially to help you improve on the skills and finger patterns frequently used by violinist and fiddlers, it is different from violin exercise methods. Carol Ann has developed and used these exercises in her own performances. I have used them, and we have taught them in workshops. We've seen people get results.

Your contribution is to dedicate a few minutes of each practice session to the improvement of technique. By following Carol Ann's instructions and advice, you can use these exercises to move closer to your goal of clarity, nimbleness, and beautiful tone.

Linda Danielson

Introduction

Warm—Ups for the Violinist is not for the sophisticated violinist with years of classical training. It has been created especially for the more casual player who is sincerely interested in getting maximum benefit from a minimum of effort.

Several years ago, after having played fiddle for about 10 years, I noticed that many similar finger patterns were repeated in the different tunes. I was aware from 20 years' experience in the violin world, prior to my fiddle experience, that there were literally miles of scales and exercises to aid the violinist in developing technique. Nothing existed in the fiddle world to help fiddlers develop technique.

Warm—Ups for the Violinist helps to fill this need. I first tested these scales and exercises on myself for six months, faithfully using them for about 20 minutes as warm—ups to my daily practice. I was rewarded with a definite improvement in my technique. I was actually surprised to see my dexterity grow as I charted my metronomic progress on a calendar. I remember thinking, "I will never be able to play faster than this." But then a couple of weeks later I would indeed climb a notch higher!

Through the years I have used these exercises in countless fiddle workshops and with private students. The letters of thanks and positive feedback from students who were thrilled with improved fiddle technique have brought me great satisfaction.

Progress with these exercises is like the progress of a body builder. Body builders do not get up in the morning and think, "I am going to develop and build my muscles today," and instantly look like Mr. Atlas. It takes weeks, months and for some, years, to attain results. It must be done over a period of time. Like all diets and exercise programs, determination and dedication are most important to success!

I sincerely believe that these exercises, when faithfully practiced, will help violinists improve their playing skills. The exercises will help develop and strengthen muscles used for finger dexterity, clarity of notes, tone, bowing–arm control, intonation, double stops, and a flexible bowing–arm wrist.

Finding JOY in doing your daily practice and patience with yourself, I believe, will be two more secrets to your success. I wish you well!

Most sincerely,

Carol Ann

How to Get the Most Out of
Warm–Ups for the Violinist

✓ Your first goal is to use this book to learn the exercises. They are not difficult when played slowly, but become more challenging as you play them at higher tempos.

✓ Be sure to study all directions and learning tips, and highlight those that are especially important and pertinent to your personal needs.

✓ After you have learned the notes, then use your own metronome to aid you in keeping a steady tempo, and begin pushing yourself to higher speeds. However, please, never make **speed** your most important goal, but rather think **quality first**!

✓ When you can play at the metronome markings in the book, then you are ready for the next step, playing along with me on the recording. At this point, having the exercises memorized allows you to concentrate more on technique.

✓ Note that there are two sets of metronome markings: one for Low–Impact Warm–Ups and another for High–Impact Warm–Ups. Also, some of the exercises are not played until the High–Impact section. So this method is like two exercise programs in one!

✓ If you enjoy variety in your practice, you can be creative in the use of your book and recording. Some days you can use the method as designed, playing along with the recording. Some may benefit from customizing the program, i.e., spending most of your time on personal "target areas" by repeating certain exercises that will help your personal needs.

When High–Impact Warm–Ups no longer presents a challenge for you, then, with the aid of your metronome, continue to build your speed.

 Make a metronome one of your best friends. It helps keep track of your progress. Write the numbers from your metronome on a calendar. You will be able to see your progress as you reach higher numbers.

 Wearing earphones when playing along with the recording is a great learning aid.

 I do not expect you to be able to keep up with me on all the exercises. At first, just listen and move your fingers (not your bow) as best you can for that portion of the recording. With time, you will be able to play up to speed.

 Please do your exercise program first when doing your daily practice. Then follow with your tunes.

 Metronome markings are ♩ = one beat unless noted otherwise.

Special note: Please take your time learning the exercises. Go for quality! Don't be a "note gobbler." That is a person who just learns the notes. Notes are not enough! It's the attention to details like good tone, intonation, timing, clarity and accuracy that will give you maximun benefit from this program.

Table of Contents

CD Contents

9

Warm–Ups for the Violinist!
Exercise #1: Dexterity

Purpose: to strengthen all fingers (especially the "pinky"!) and to promote speed, dexterity, and clarity of all four fingers.

Technique Check–Off List

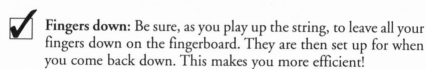 **Fingers down:** Be sure, as you play up the string, to leave all your fingers down on the fingerboard. They are then set up for when you come back down. This makes you more efficient!

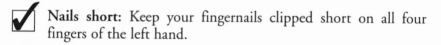 **Nails short:** Keep your fingernails clipped short on all four fingers of the left hand.

Fingers on tips: Play on the tips of your fingers, not the sides. This makes your notes cleaner.

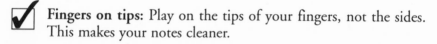 **Arm under:** If your fingers sound flat or seem too short, make sure that your left elbow is under the fiddle. This makes your fingers longer.

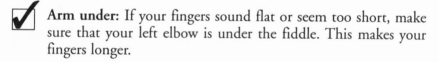 **Left thumb:** Do not allow your left thumb to come up higher than 1/2 to 3/4 inch above your fingerboard. (Your thumb will change its position as you change strings.)

Close action: Strive to keep your fingers close to the fingerboard and relaxed.

Wrist straight: Do not allow your wrist to bend or collapse, as this keeps fingers from being on their tips. It also makes vibrato more difficult and shifting to the higher register almost impossible.

Repeat the dexterity exercise on all four strings at different speeds. Start at a tempo on your metronome that is comfortable for you, then build up your speed at your own pace, until you can keep up with me on the recording.

As soon as you are feeling comfortable with the notes and have them memorized, begin using the **alternate bowing pattern**. I nicknamed it this because it alternates between two notes together (in one bow) and two notes separate.

Think: "two together, two alone, two together, two alone." This is a very common style of bowing pattern used by fiddlers and violinist. It will help you sound less choppy ("saw–saw") and more smooth.

Learning tip: Using Finger Patterns
Notice how I have used "Pattern #1," "Pattern#2," etc., in the dexterity exercise. These refer to groups or patterns of fingers that occur in the exercise. Note how many times a pattern repeats itself. Finger patterns also occur in fiddle tunes, and I find them very useful when learning and playing tunes.

Track #
2 & 26

1A. Dexterity on the G String with Single Bowing Pattern

Low Impact: The metronome is set at 84. (♩ = one beat,

♩ = one beat, ○ = one beat)

High Impact cut #26: The metronome is set at 92. (♩ = one beat.
○ = one beat)

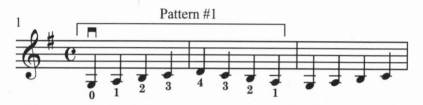

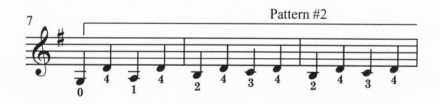

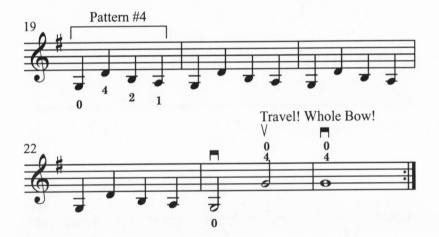

Low Impact: Repeat 3 times, doubling the tempo each time.
High Impact: Play twice. Double the tempo the second time.

1B. Dexterity on the D String
with Alternate Bowing Pattern

Low Impact: The metronome is set at 92. ($\downarrow$ = one beat,
$\circ$ = one beat,)

High Impact cut #27: The metronome is set at 104. ($\downarrow$ = one beat,
$\circ$ = one beat)

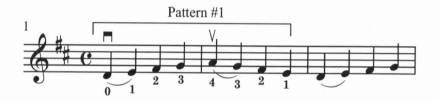

Pattern #3

Pattern #4

Travel! Whole Bow!

Play twice.
Double the tempo the second time.

1C. Dexterity on the E String with Alternate Bowing Pattern

Low Impact: The metronome is set at 96. ($\downarrow$ = one beat, $\mathbf{o}$ = one beat,)

High Impact cut #28: The metronome is set at 112. ($\downarrow$ = one beat, $\mathbf{o}$ = one beat)

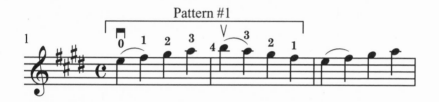

16

Play twice.
Double the tempo the second time.

Exercise #2: The 60–Second Bow

No written music is possible for this exercise. When it is performed correctly, it does not necessarily "sound" good. If someone hears you playing it they will wonder, "What are you doing?" For this reason many people do not think of it as "fun to do," however, when done faithfully it really does work! Make a commitment to yourself to try it for one full month, and then "see and feel" the results. This exercise will help improve your tone for waltzes, airs, and other slow tunes plus you will gain better control of your bowing arm muscles. This means everything you play sounds better!

Purpose: To strengthen and develop control of the muscles in the right bowing arm. Strength and better control of these arm muscles will help you develop fuller, richer tone (rather than shaky muscles which produce a shaky tone.)

Bow Preparation: If you happen to have a second bow it is nice to use it as an "exercise bow". If not, it is fine to mark your regular bow. Using five small pieces of masking tape, use the tape to "mark" and divide your bow into six, exactly equal sections as illustrated below in figure #1:

10 Seconds 10 Sec. 10 Sec. 10 Sec. 10 Sec. 10 Sec.

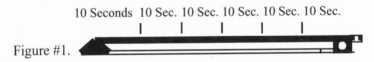

Figure #1.

Step one: Using one full bow stroke, take 15 seconds to move from exactly where your frog begins to the very tip of your bow. Do not worry about the volume or the quality of your tone at this point. What you are trying to do is produce a continuous sound (Fig. #2).

Figure #2.

←————————15 Sec.————————→

Step two: This time, using one full bow stroke, make your bow stroke last 30 seconds. Your tone will be smaller now, but don't worry about this at all. Do turn your attention however to making whatever tone or "sound" you do have as smooth as possible, and continuous. Try not to let it stop or jerk.

Figure #3.

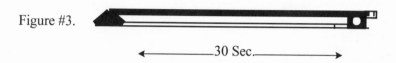

Step three: You can take a couple of weeks, if you choose, to build up to this next goal which is your final goal: the "60 Second Bow" using one bow stroke. Again, please do not concern yourself with the quality of tone or the volume. Your sound will be very small, almost barely audible. Your goal is to make it as smooth and continuous as possible, with as few jerks or "holes" in the sound. You want a non–stop flow of sound. Try to "spend" (move) your bow so slowly that you use 10 seconds between each marked sections of your bow (Fig. #4).

Figure #4.

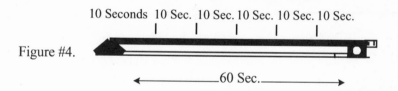

Do the exercise (on any of your strings) one time using a down bow, and the next time start (at the tip) with an up bow. Even two minutes per day on this exercise will help you develop control of your right–arm muscles. For those wishing faster results, you could do it twice on each string (one down bow, one up) for a total of eight bows. However I recommend you do no more then two bow strokes, then change to another activity or tune, then in five or ten minutes come back and repeat the exercise. This will prevent over tiring the arm muscles. Please be sure to relax your arm muscles for a few seconds at the completion of each stroke.

The 60–Second Bow

Metronome = 60

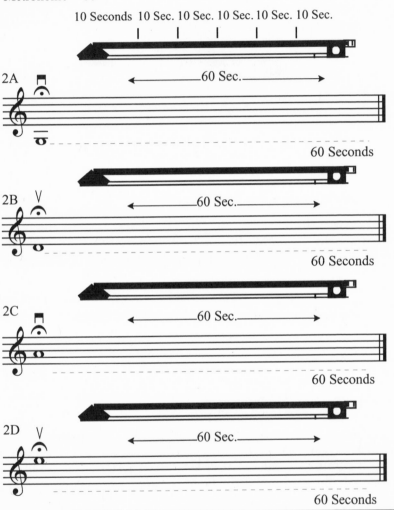

Important: Be sure to use <u>EVERY</u> SINGLE INCH of your bow. You will start exactly down at the "frog" of the bow (right where the metal starts), barely moving very slowly, taking 60 seconds to reach the tip of your bow.

Exercise #3: The Triplet Exercise

Purpose: to develop quick, nimble, "snappy" finger action and clarity of notes.

This is one of my favorite warm–ups. Triplet figures occur frequently in fiddle and violin music. This exercise will help you "pop your notes out" and make them clean and clear. It will also help you develop your fingers for grace notes or embellishments that are used in many styles of fiddling as well as violin.

Relaxation: In this triplet exercise and in all of the exercises requiring left–hand finger movement... strive for a new awareness of relaxation in your left-hand fingers. When they get tired, stiff, and tense, fatigue sets in, and with fatigue comes mistakes.

Most fiddlers and violinist need to <u>learn to relax</u>.

Special instructions: Be sure to give a slight accent or, as I call it, "bite" to the *first* note of each set of triplets. Play the exercise twice through to count as one time.

Chart your progress. It can be satisfying to keep track of your progress by marking down on a calendar the tempo settings from your metronome. Determination will pay off!

Exercise #3: The Triplet Exercise

Low Impact: The metronome is set at 72, 84, 96, and 104. (♩ = one beat)

High Impact cut #29: The metronome = 88, 100 - cut #30, 108 - cut #31. (♩ = one beat)

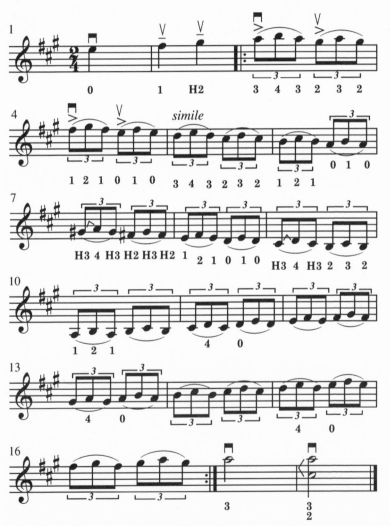

Exercise #4: The Vibrato Exercise

Purpose: to create a time in your practice period that you concentrate on developing your vibrato and acquire the skill to produce different speeds of vibrato.

Since I had already played violin for 20 years prior to entering the fiddle world, I already knew and used vibrato. It was my observation, however, that many of the top fiddlers used a slower vibrato in the old time fiddle world. I decided to make my vibrato slower. I found this very difficult for me, in fact, almost impossible!

I began sitting or standing in front of a mirror, watching my left hand. I found that I had to just play the simplest of notes such as a G scale. I could then really concentrate on the movement of my left hand. I found that an unmetered scale allowed me to stay on one finger as long as I needed to develop the speed I wanted. As I watched my fingers, I visualized in my mind those fiddlers with the slow vibrato. I personally admired them very much and tried to achieve that same look in my left hand.

I feel that slowing down my vibrato was difficult for me because I entered the "fiddle world" with a "violin style" of vibrato that had been ingrained in me for 20 years. Now I feel much better about my vibrato. It really did take a lot of time and perseverance on my part. If you have spent a long time in the "violin world" with a fast intense vibrato, you may find this a challenge as I did, but if you wish to aquire the ability to change vibrato speeds, this exercise will help you.

Note: For this exercise it is assumed that you already know how to do vibrato. If not, this is a technique difficult to learn from a book, and I would strongly urge you to take some private lessons or get some help from someone who knows how to do vibrato.

Instructions: Simply play an unmetered G scale, playing the open string notes twice, first with your fourth finger then followed by an open string where you relax the muscles in your left hand, then continue on up the scale. If you feel like you need more time or practice on any particular finger, feel free to spend several seconds remaining on that finger.

Exercise #4:
The Vibrato Exercise

Unmetered, Two Octave, Modified G Scale

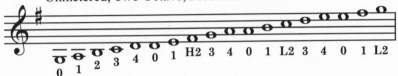

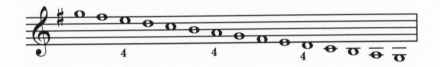

Vibrato Check–Off List

 Relax: Keep sending the message from your brain down your arm to your left hand to relax! One of the secrets to vibrato is to relax.

 Two points of contact: There will be two places where your left hand "touches" (has contact with) your fiddle:
#1. The finger on which you are vibrating
#2. Your left thumb (against the neck of the fiddle)

For example, if you are using vibrato on the second finger, then be sure to lift your first finger off! This will give you more freedom of movement to do vibrato.

Think: Two secrets to vibrato are freedom and relaxation!

 Spend time: Feel free to spend as much time as you like on each note.

 Mirror: Looking at your left hand in a mirror is a great learning and practice technique. A three way mirror is great for observing your fingers doing vibrato.

 Speed: Are you able to change the speed of your vibrato at will? Some waltzes, like slow lyrical waltzes, and slower sections of violin music, are enhanced by a slower vibrato. The more "old–timey," up–tempo waltzes sound best with a faster vibrato.

 Intonation: Notice that when you play the open string *(following the same note played with the fourth finger)* you have a chance to check your intonation of the fourth finger. You can also relax the muscles of your left hand.

Exercise #5: The Chromatic Exercise

The word "chromatic" means moving by half step. Short chromatic "licks" occur frequently in fiddle tunes and violin music, so this is a really good skill to develop.

Purpose: to develop the ability to move from one note to another in a chromatic passage with clean notes, not smeared notes.

Instructions: Play the exercise through three times, doubling the tempo with each repeat.

1. First time = separate bows.
2. Second time = twice as fast, again with separate bows.
3. Third time = again, double the speed but use one long
slurred bow.

To "slur" means to play more than one note per bow. This is indicated in music with a curved line enclosing two or more notes. In playing the exercise the third time, there will be a total of eight notes all in one bow going up and eight notes all in one bow going down.

Special instructions: Repeat this chromatic exercise on all four strings, using the same fingering and the same bowings on all strings. Practice the entire exercise at the same tempo. When ready, increase the tempo using each notch of your metronome. This will occur over a period of time. It would be good to review slower tempos as you progress to the faster tempos.

5A. Chromatic Exercise on the G String

Play 3 times – doubling the tempo each time.
Low Impact: Metronome = 69
High Impact cut #32: Metronome = 100. Play ALL FOUR strings NON–STOP.

1st time = Separate Bowing

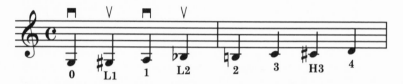

2nd Time = Separate Bowing

3rd Time = Slur one bow up and one bow down.

5B. Chromatic Exercise on the D String

Play 3 times – Doubling the tempo each time.
Low Impact: Metronome = 80.
High Impact cut #32: Metronome = 100.

1st Time = Separate Bowing

2nd time = Separate bowing

3rd time = Slur one bow up and one bow down

Learning tip:
Remember, clean transition between notes, not smeared.

29

Track
13

5C. Chromatic Exercise
on the A String

Same directions – same fingering
Low Impact: The metronome = 88.

5D. Chromatic Exercise on the E String

Low Impact: The metronome = 96.

Exercise #6: The Wrist Exercise

Purpose: to develop a relaxed, fluid, flexible wrist.

Since a large majority of old time fiddle and violin music is playing fast notes and changing strings quickly, using the wrist (rather than the whole bowing arm) will help make you a more efficient fiddler. A flexible wrist and arm are very important. Be sure to create a spot in your practice time for this exercise if you feel any stiffness.

Instructions: You will repeat the exercise at least three times, thinking of your strings as "pairs". For example, the G & D are the bottom pair, the D and A, the middle pair.

Begin playing slowly, using big bows, gradually increasing the speed, using smaller bows as you gain speed. Use an indefinite number of notes.

The Wrist Exercise

Wrist Check–Off List

✓ **Look:** Actually look at your wrist both directly (your eyes looking at your arm) and indirectly by looking in the mirror (your eyes looking in a mirror at your arm).

✓ **Think:** "Wrist relax!"

✓ **Think:** "Hand drop...hand lift." You should see your right hand drop and lift.

✓ **Realize:** The bow will actually "tilt" as you lift and drop to change strings.

✓ **Wrist, not arm!** Change strings by using your wrist, not your arm.

✓ **Bow size:** Please remember to apply one of my golden rules when playing this exercise:

Golden Rule:
    The faster you go, the smaller you bow.

Exercise #7: Open–String "Roll–Ups"

The term "roll–ups" is a nickname I coined for little, short, "scale–like" licks that frequently occur in fiddling.

Purpose: To develop nimbleness and lightness in your fingers so that when you come across these little scales in a tune, they will be executed (not murdered!) with clean, clear precision and not blurred or smeared together.

Instructions: Practice this exercise at slow, medium and fast tempos so that you will be prepared for all applications. Think, regarding your notes, "Tum–ble–them–out! Tum–ble–them–out!" Try tapping just your fingers, not your bow, on the fingerboard. They should be able to make little "snapping" sounds as they lightly "snap" down on the strings. Use the same fingerings on all four strings.

7A. Roll–Ups on the G String

Low Impact: Metronome = 80.
High Impact cut #33: Metronome = 100. All four strings non stop.

Track # 17

Special Instructions:

Repeat 4 times at slow speed.
Repeat 4 times at medium speed.
Repeat 8 times at fast speed.

Wrist Check–Off List

 "Snap"! Snap your fingers to the fingerboard when playing roll-ups.

 Relax: Relax your fingering muscles immediately following the effort of snapping your fingers down.

 Close action: Keep the fingers close to the fingerboard when playing roll-ups. Use an efficient motion.

7B. Roll–Ups on the D String

Low Impact: The metronome = 88.

7C. Roll–Ups on the A String

Low Impact: The metronome is set at 96.

7D. Roll–Ups on the E String

Low Impact: The metronome is set at 104.

Exercise #8. First–Finger Roll–Ups

YOU WILL FIND EXERCISE #8
IN THE HIGH–IMPACT WARM–UPS
SECTION–cut #34
Delete when playing LOW–IMPACT

Instructions: When you can do Exercise 7 beginning on open strings, then add to your collection of "roll–ups" by starting on the first finger. Play non–stop on all four strings.

High Impact: Metronome = 104. ($\flat$ = one beat)

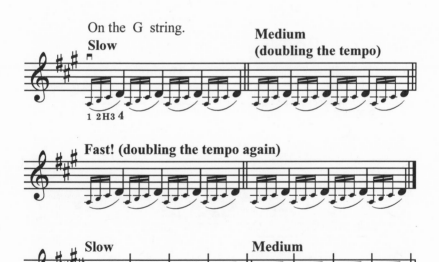

Slow ... **Medium**

Fast!

Slow ... **Medium**

Fast!

Exercise #9: The Double–Stop Exercise Adding Fingers First to the Upper String

Purpose: to familiarize your fingers with the correct intonation of common double stops that occur in fiddle tunes. An additional purpose is to memorize the "feel" (kinesthetic memory) of the correct intervals (distance between the two pitches). A third goal is to develop finger coordination: that is, using two different fingers on two different strings at the same time with good intonation.

The phrase "double stop" refers to playing on two strings at the same time. It could be open strings, or there may be fingers involved. When two fingers are used on two strings, it becomes more difficult. This exercise will help prepare you for the simpler frequently used combinations that occur in violin music. Please keep in mind that playing the double stops with fingers on the correct strings is not enough. They need to be in tune!

 Make sure that your violin is perfectly in tune.

Instructions: Do the exercise two different ways. First (the easier way) add your fingers to the upper string as in Exercise 9A.

The marking > indicates a half step. The fingers are close to each other.

9A. Double–Stop Exercise

Play 3 times – doubling the tempo each time.
Low Impact: On the bottom pair of strings. Metronome = 66
High Impact cut #35: Play all three pairs of strings non–stop.
Metronome = 84

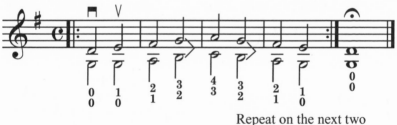

Repeat on the next two
pairs of strings.

As you change strings the instructions, fingering, and spacing remains the same. You may "feel" a different sensation in the left hand because the angle of the hand changes slightly as you move from one pair of strings to the next.

9B. Double–Stop Exercise

Low Impact: On the middle pair of strings.
The metronome = 72

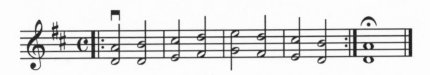

9C. Double–Stop Exercise

Low Impact: On the top pair of strings. The metronome = 80

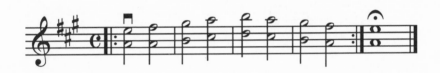

9D. Double–Stop Exercise Adding Fingers First to the Lower Strings

> **YOU WILL FIND EXERCISE #9D
> IN THE HIGH–IMPACT WARM–UPS SECTION**
> Delete when playing LOW–IMPACT

When you are able to play the Exercise 9A, adding your fingers to the upper string first, then, you are ready for a challenge! Add your fingers to the lower strings first, as below in Exercise 9D. This creates a new series of double stops.

Track
36

Play each section 3 times – doubling the tempo each time.
High Impact cut #36: Metronome = 84

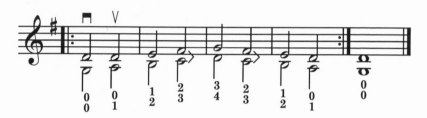

Continue on non–stop to the next two pairs of strings.

Please remember:
Your first goal is accuracy of intonation, so do not
play too fast too soon. Speed will come with time.
Accuracy **now**, speed **later!**

Exercise #10: The "Turnaround"

Fiddlers call a commonly used pattern of notes a "lick." The lick in Exercise #10 we'll call a "turnaround." You will find turnarounds in abundance in fiddle and violin music, both with an upward and downward movement, so our exercise includes both patterns. The better you can play this exercise, the better these little patterns will sound in your playing.

Purpose: to develop a nimbleness in the fingers and comfort with the turnaround patterns as they occur in fiddle and violin music. Exercise #10 will raise this comfort to such a level that your brain does not compute the notes on an individual basis, i.e., 3, 2, 1, 3, but rather as groups of notes. For those of you that type, the concept of "speed words" or "flash words" (i.e., you think of the word as a whole, rather than the individual letters of the word) may be helpful.

Instructions: First learn the notes of the basic exercise. Second, add the accents and bowing as indicated. Third, when you can play with good intonation, accents and bowing, begin building speed with your metronome and by playing along with the instruction CD.

Learning tip reminders: Strive for:

 Close finger action

 Feeling of relaxation

 "The faster you go, the smaller you bow"

10A. The Turnaround Starting on Open G String– Single Noting

Low Impact: Metronome = 72. (♩ = one beat)
High Impact cut #37: Metronome = 92. Play twice–doubling tempo second time. (♩ = one beat, ♪ = one beat)

10B. The Turnaround
Using Alternate Bowing Pattern

Low Impact: Metronome = 80
High Impact cut #38: Metronome = 100. ♩ = one beat

10C. The Turnaround Using Alternate Bowing Pattern–Accenting on the Beat

Low Impact: Metronome = 92.
High Impact cut #39: Metronome = 104. ($\quad$ = one beat)
    Proceed on to Exercise #10d.

This completes your LOW–IMPACT WARM–UPS program. Continue using the Low–Impact Warm–Ups for as long as you feel you are benefiting from it. When in the course of your personal fitness program, you no longer feel challenged, then you're ready to graduate to the HIGH–IMPACT WARM–UPS. High Impact Exercises begin at cut #26 (page 12) on your CD.

This completes the Low–Impact section of *Warm–Ups for the Violinist*. Please take as much time as you feel you need to learn the exercises in the Low–Impact Warm–Ups section. This will vary with each student. When you begin to feel comfortable with the exercises and tempos, and they no longer present a challenge for you, then you are ready to graduate to High–Impact.

Instructions for High–Impact Warm–Ups

Now begin the book again, starting on page 12, but use the new tempo markings for High–Impact and practice the exercises at faster more challenging tempos.

Your final goal is to play along with me in the High-Impact section of the *Warm–Ups for the Violinist* recording. Some of the exercises may have a large tempo jump from one metronome number to the next. If you have trouble keeping up, you may want to set your metronome for smaller jumps, and work up to the fastest tempo.

In closing, please remember that in any exercise or fitness program, *discipline, dedication, and determination* are crucial to success. You will get out of this program what you put into it. This program has helped me with my own technique, and I have seen it work for countless students. It can also work for you! The better you can do these exercises, the better you will be able to play your violin music.

Wishing you success and continued enjoyment of your music!

Most sincerely,

Carol Ann

10D. The Turnaround
Using Alternating Bowing
Pattern–Accenting off the Beat

High Impact cut #40: Metronome = 108. ($\quad$ = one beat)

51

Exercise #11: The Two–String Scale

Purpose: to develop good intonation when playing double stops. To increase your comfort level with double stops.

I created this little double stop workout to help me with intonation. I was having a real intonation problem in tunes where I would play a finger on one string and then <u>add</u> to it a <u>different</u> finger on another string at the same time. This workout has helped me. It will work for you if you focus on the instructions and adhere to them (i.e. like keeping that finger <u>down</u>. Gently stretch those tendons in your left hand.) Strive for quality in intonation FIRST. Speed is your secondary goal to be reached over a period of time.

Instructions:

1) First use the music to learn the notes of the exercise. Then you are ready to play along with me. Use ear phones for part of your practice. Please do not use them all the time as your attention to YOUR OWN SOUNDS may be neglected.

2) Be aware of and memorize the relationships between your fingers. Are the fingers right next to each other? We will call this "closed position" or a half step. When there is about an inch spacing between your fingers, it is a whole step, and we will call this "open position." You should know before you put your fingers down, are you going for closed or open? Don't just guess. Decide <u>what</u> you want to play, then do it.

Play the exercise four times;

1) Play whole notes.
2) Play half notes.
3) Play quarter notes.
4) Play quarter notes with alternate bowing pattern.

Learning tips:
1) **Your fiddle** *must* be *perfectly* **in tune.** This is crucial. You are memorizing the **feel** and the **sound** of the correct spacing of the fingers. If the relationship between the strings is altered, then the spacing of the fingers will be altered.

2) Keep your fingers on their tips. This prevents you from touching other strings. You will also get a cleaner tone by using the firmer tips of the fingers as opposed to the fleshier side.

3) The line following the number 4 (4————————) indicates that you **leave down** your fourth finger. You may feel a stretching sensation in the fingers. This means you are getting some good bonus results from the exercise.

11A. The Two–String Scale on the Middle Pair of Strings

Since double-stop combinations occur on different combinations of strings, it is important to practice this exercise on all three pairs of strings. The fingerings and the distance between the fingers will remain the same. As you change pairs of strings, the angle of the hand will change, and you may experience a different sensation or feeling of stretch in your left hand.

YOU WILL FIND EXERCISE #11A IN THE HIGH–IMPACT WARM–UPS SECTION

High Impact cut #41: Metronome = 76

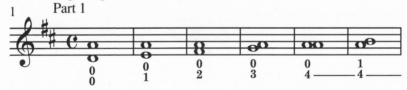

Part 2

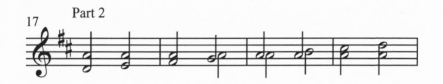

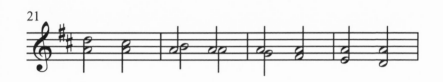

Part 3

11B. The Two–String Scale on the Top Pair of Strings

As you feel more comfortable with the notes in this exercise you can add to your goals. When you are feeling good about your accuracy of intonation you can raise your goals to include TONE and an awareness of your body. Merely playing the double stops will no longer be enough. You now will strive to play with EASE, so that the tone "flows" out of your violin. You wish to feel RELAXED as you play. Strive to make it LOOK easy, SOUND easy, and <u>FEEL</u> easy!

YOU WILL FIND EXERCISE #11B IN THE HIGH–IMPACT WARM–UPS SECTION

High Impact cut #42: Metronome = 88.
Part 1

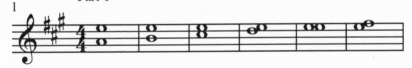

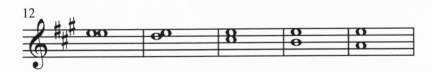

Exercise #12A: The Turnaround Starting on First Finger on the G String

> **YOU WILL FIND EXERCISE #12A IN THE HIGH–IMPACT WARM–UPS SECTION**

Here's a variation on the Turnaround Exercise. When we started on the G string, we played the exercise in the key of G. Now we will begin on the first finger on the G string. This will change the exercise into the key of A, a very popular key, and give a new set of finger patterns that will include a HIGH third finger on the G and D strings. All directions from Exercise #10 still apply.

12A. The Turnaround Starting on First Finger on the G String

High Impact cut #43: Metronome = 92 ♪ = one beat
Play twice – doubling tempo second time – ♩ = one beat

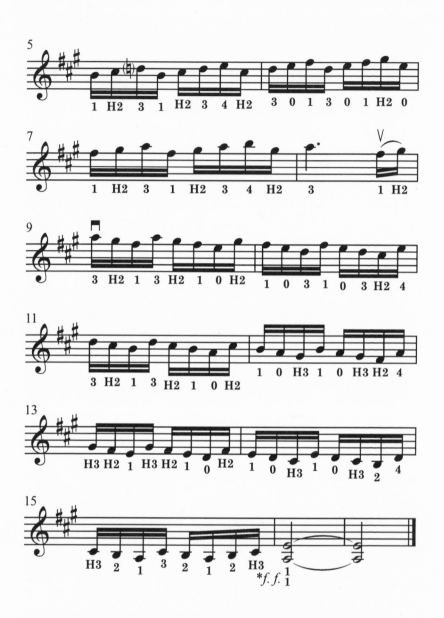

f.f. - Stands for "fat finger." This is a nickname I use when one finger is on two strings at the same time. The finger will be more on its side rather than its tip, hence it is "fatter."

12B. The Turnaround Using Alternate Bowing Pattern– Accenting *off* the Beat

High Impact cut #44: Metronome = 100.

Track
45

12C. The Turnaround Using Alternate Bowing Pattern– Accenting *on* the Beat

High Impact cut #45: Metronome = 108.